The Let's Talk Library™

Let's Talk About Nightmares

Melanie Ann Apel

The Rosen Publishing Group's
PowerKids Press™
New York

To Michael B. Bonnell, for making my nightmares go away and making my dreams come true.
All my love forever.

Published in 2002 by The Rosen Publishing Group, Inc.
29 East 21st Street, New York, NY 10010

First Edition

Book Layout: Emily Muschinske

Project Editor: Jennifer Quasha

Photo Credits: all photos by Joseph J. Muschinske

Apel, Melanie Ann.
   Let's talk about nightmares / Melanie Ann Apel.—1st ed.
   — (The let's talk library)
Includes index.
   ISBN 0-8239-5860-4
1. Children's dreams—Juvenile literature. 2. Nightmares—Juvenile literature. [1. Dreams. 2. Nightmares.]
I. Title. II. Series.
   BF1099.C55 A64 2001
154.6'32—dc21
                                                                00-011239

Manufactured in the United States of America

Contents

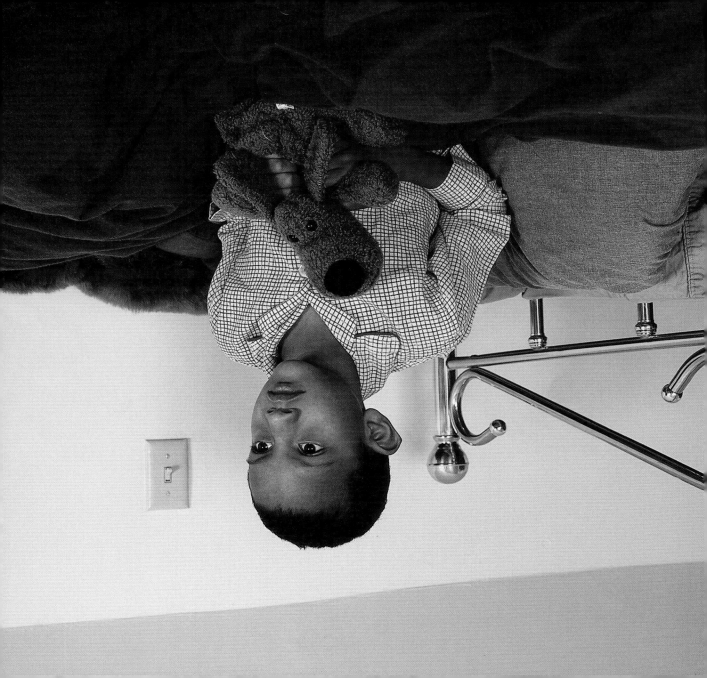

David's Bad Dream

Every night David snuggles into his bed. He pulls the covers up tight. He hugs his teddy bear and closes his eyes. Soon David drifts off to sleep. Most nights David sleeps through the night and wakes up ready for a new day. Sometimes he dreams about things that happened during the day. Sometimes he dreams about exciting adventures. Not all of David's dreams are sweet, though. Sometimes David has a bad dream. The dream might be so upsetting that it wakes him up in the middle of the night.

◀ *Nightmares are scary dreams.*

What Are Nightmares?

Everyone dreams when they sleep. You may not remember all of your dreams. Most dreams are about everyday things like playing with your friends or going to school. Have you ever had a dream that was scary? These types of dreams are called nightmares. Some people wake up when they have a nightmare. Some nightmares just **disturb** your sleep. Everyone has nightmares once in a while. Even big kids and grownups have nightmares. If you have nightmares, you are not alone.

Hannah is sleeping peacefully. ▶

Why Do You Dream?

Dreaming is an important and healthy part of sleeping. When you dream, your mind is working through **situations** and problems in your everyday life. Most dreams are pleasant. If your mother is going to have a baby, you might dream about what it will be like to be a big brother or sister. You should make sure to get enough sleep so you have time to dream. Without enough sleep and time to dream, you could feel very cranky when morning comes.

◀ *Nightmares are a part of growing up.*

Jenny's Nightmare

Last night Jenny watched a scary movie on television with her sister Julie. They watched the movie with the lights off. Both girls were scared before they went to sleep. Jenny woke up crying in the middle of the night. She had a dream about things she and Julie saw in the scary movie on television. Sometimes people have nightmares because of something **frightening** that they saw.

Watching a scary movie before bedtime can cause a nightmare. ▶

Rakim's Fears

Sometimes you have nightmares when a bad thing has happened in your life. Lately, Rakim has been having a lot of nightmares. Rakim's grandmother died a month ago and he misses her very much. He is also afraid that he will lose other people he loves, the way he lost his grandmother. Rakim thinks about this when he is at school. That makes it hard for him to concentrate on what the teacher is saying. At home he stays close to his father and brother because he worries about them, too. Sometimes these scary thoughts give Rakim nightmares.

◀ *Fear can creep up on you while you are doing something else.*

How to Deal with Nightmares

What should you do when a nightmare wakes you? Try to go back to sleep if you can. If you can't sleep, you may need comfort. Holding your favorite stuffed animal may make you feel better. You may need to wake up someone to comfort you. Ask an adult to sit with you until you are no longer afraid and can fall back to sleep. It might help to talk about the nightmare and why it scared you. Even if you do not feel like talking, having someone nearby who loves you can make all the difference in the world.

Getting a hug from someone you love will help you feel better if you have a nightmare. ▶

Talking It Out

If something bad has happened recently or if there are a lot of changes going on in your life, you might have more nightmares than usual. Facing many changes at once might make you feel **anxious**, and this feeling could lead to nightmares. One way to handle feeling anxious is to talk to someone. Talking can help you see that you are not the only one who has nightmares when you are worried. Once you talk to someone, your fears seem a lot easier to handle.

17

◀ *Rakim talks to his mom about his nightmares.*

Feeling Less Afraid at Bedtime

There are things that you can do to make yourself feel less afraid at bedtime. Having a night-light in your room may make you feel better. Maybe sleeping with the bedroom door open a little bit or bringing a blanket and teddy bear to bed might help. If you're worried about nightmares, don't watch or read anything scary before going to sleep. Choose whatever **ritual** works best for you. If you want, you can try them all. The important thing is to feel better and to try to keep away nightmares.

Reading a happy story before bedtime helps take away nightmares. ▶

Talk Back to Your Nightmare

Suzy saw snakes at the zoo and they frightened her. When Suzy wakes up from a nightmare about snakes, her mom sits and comforts her. She tells her that she is safe. Together they talk about how Suzy can make the snakes go away. Suzy's mom says, "Tell those snakes to go home!" She tells her this a few times and then asks Suzy to try it for herself. "Go home, snakes!" Suzy says. Before she goes back to sleep, Suzy's mom reminds her that if she has another nightmare about snakes she should tell those snakes to just go home!

◀ *Suzy feels better when she talks back to her nightmare.*

A Good Night's Rest

Even though it is hard to have nightmares, remember that everyone has them. The important thing is to try to make yourself feel better. Talk to someone about the scary things that happened in your nightmare. Use a night-light or bring a teddy bear or blanket to bed with you. Try talking back to your nightmare when you have one. If your nightmares have to do with a difficult situation in your life, try to work on the problem. That will show you how things that seem so scary are not really that scary once you take a good look at them.

Glossary

anxious (AYNK-shus) Feeling uneasy or worried.

disturb (dih-STERB) To interrupt or disrupt.

frightening (FRYT-en-ing) Very scary.

ritual (RIH-choo-ul) Something that you do regularly.

situations (sih-choo-AY-shunz) Places or settings.

Index